01/1916

D1009739

KEEPING Amphibians

A PRACTICAL GUIDE TO CARING FOR FROGS, TOADS, NEWTS, AND SALAMANDERS

ANDREW R. GRAY

First edition for the United States, Canada, and the Philippine Republic published by Barron's Educational Series, Inc., 2001.

Originally published in English by HarperCollins*Publishers* Ltd. under the title:
COLLINS UNUSUAL PETS: KEEPING AMPHIBIANS
Text and design © HarperCollins*Publishers* Ltd., 2000
Photographs © David Manning, 2000
Illustrations © Felicity Rose Cole, 2000

All inquiries should be addressed to:
Barron's Educational Series, Inc.
250 Wireless Boulevard
Hauppauge, New York 11788
http://www.barronseduc.com

Library of Congress Catalog Card No. 00-107172

International Standard Book No. 0-7641-1759-9

9 8 7 6 5 4 3 2 1

Designer: Colin Brown
Photography: Animal Ark, London, apart from pp.4, 40, and 54.
Illustrations: Felicity Rose Cole

Color reproduction by Colourscan, Singapore
Printed and bound by Printing Express Ltd, Hong Kong

Please Note
While every reasonable care was taken in the compilation of this publication, the publisher and author cannot accept liability for any loss, damage, injury, or death resulting from the keeping of amphibians by user(s) of this publication, or from the use of any materials, equipment, methods, or information recommended in this publication or from any errors or omissions that may be found in the text of this publication or that may occur at a future date, except as expressly provided by law.

Dedication

I wrote this book especially to dedicate it to Laurie Smith. He nurtured my interest in animals from an early age and has always been there for me to show how much he cares.

Thank you very much, Loz, for everything you have ever done for me, and my family.
Love, Andrew

Contents

Introduction

Amphibians include some of the most beautiful and fascinating of all living creatures. Many have lifestyles and behavior that make them very interesting to keep, and they can give an enormous amount of pleasure and satisfaction. This book will help you to choose an amphibian to keep, and give you advice on how to care for your chosen species.

This book is intended as a simple guide to keeping amphibians. The first sections cover the basic requirements and general principles involved in keeping amphibians successfully. It is important that you study these principles and understand what each species requires in terms of equipment, space, and maintenance before you attempt to keep any of the amphibians. The different species have been organized in an ease-of-care order, with the easiest to keep appearing first.

Choosing an amphibian

There is a great variety of different amphibians that make excellent pets. When deciding which species to choose, spend some time finding out more about the ones that interest you now, and will hold your interest in the future. You may have your amphibian for a long time, as some species can live for up to 16 years in captivity.

Watching nocturnal amphibians, like this attractive tree frog, can give hours of pleasure.

Many amphibians are nocturnal; for some people who are busy during the day, being able to watch their animal's activities in the evening is a definite advantage.

Although most amphibians are relatively small, it is important to consider the lifestyle of a particular species when you select the size of suitable housing. Some large amphibians prefer to remain in one place, hardly moving from one day to the next. These may be content to live in a small container, whereas other, smaller but highly active and agile species will need much more room. Many species prefer to be kept in pairs or groups, but care should be taken not to overcrowd a vivarium or aquarium as this can cause unhealthy and stressful conditions.

When obtaining more than one animal, it is always a good idea to try to determine the age and sex of the individuals and also to select specimens of similar sizes. Behavior may vary. Some species of frogs and certain salamanders are highly territorial and are best kept singularly.

Further details are given in each species description.

Unlike this unusual Shovel-nosed Frog, many amphibians are easy to acquire.

Where to obtain stock

Once you have decided to keep an amphibian, it is necessary to find a supplier that stocks healthy specimens, and also one that can provide all the necessary equipment and food. Specialist mail-order companies can have a wide choice of amphibians, but the main disadvantage is that you cannot see what you are buying. This is, however, a very popular way of obtaining equipment and a regular food supply for your animals. Some pet shops offer a selection of the more popular amphibian species and the more specialized shops often offer a good variety of species with advice on caring for them.

Joining a herpetological society would enable you to meet experienced hobbyists who may offer animals in good condition and also plenty of good advice.

Selecting a healthy specimen

Starting off with young, captive-bred specimens generally leads to greater success when keeping amphibians. These are usually free from disease and internal parasites and are used to life in captivity. Information relating to the age and previous care of the animal may also be available. Obtaining animals that have been born in captivity helps to reduce the number collected from the wild. Always quarantine any new amphibians before introducing them to existing stock.

Look for specimens that:
- have bright and clear eyes
- have uniform and unblemished skin coloration
- have no broken skin tissue or damage to tip of nose, mouth, or limbs
- have no sores or ulcers on their undersides
- are not too thin and that are carrying sufficient body weight
- are active and alert
- have sturdy limbs and good visible bone structure.

Healthy and well-kept amphibians are bright-eyed, alert, and have good appetites.

Handling

No amphibian enjoys being "petted" and to avoid stressing the animals, handling should be kept to a minimum. Much more pleasure can be gained from admiring their beauty and observing their behavior. Great satisfaction can also be gained in the knowledge that they are being maintained successfully.

When handling is necessary, a great amount of care must be taken as their fragile skin can easily be damaged. Generally, it is advisable to wet your hands before handling amphibians; otherwise you risk burning the animal with the heat generated by your hand. The correct handling of an amphibian depends on the species concerned, and further information on handling is given in the species descriptions. Always wash your hands thoroughly before and after handling any amphibian.

KEY

On each of the species pages there is a simple key to show at a glance the basic keeping requirements, life expectancy, and maximum size for each amphibian.

Caging

This indicates the type of home each species requires. There are 6 different types: semi-aquatic, fully aquatic, arboreal, semiarid, terrestrial, or simple.

Diet

Almost all amphibians are carnivorous (meat-eating), living on a diet of insects, spiders, worms, and other small animals. Details of specific food requirements are given in the text.

Maximum Life Span

The information shown gives a rough idea of the amphibian's life span in captivity. Many factors can affect this, including stress and disease.

Maximum Length

The size of amphibians varies considerably. The maximum length shown in the key is for females, as they normally grow larger than males.

Many amphibians would rather sit in the hand than be restrained. Cup "jumpers" in two hands.

Anatomy

Amphibians are vertebrate animals that have a skull, backbone, and ribs. They are classified by scientists into 3 groups or orders: the caecilians, the newts and salamanders, and the frogs and toads. The frogs and toads form the largest group of amphibians with over 4,000 different species. Amphibians differ widely in size, shape, and color, but they share some common characteristics.

Newts and salamanders, which live a highly aquatic existence, have elongated bodies and short limbs. Most frog species, which spend their adult life in water, also have streamlined bodies and heavily webbed feet, whereas land species tend to have rounder bodies and little or no webbing. Many species of amphibians lay their eggs in water. These then develop into the familiar tadpoles or larvae before changing (metamorphosing) into the adult amphibian.

climb on smooth, slippery surfaces. Amphibian limbs usually have four digits, or fingers, on the front legs and five on the hind, although this can vary among species. Salamanders and tadpoles can regenerate lost limbs.

External features

Limbs

Frogs that jump have long, powerful hind legs. Climbing species, such as tree frogs, have expanded toe-pads, helping them to

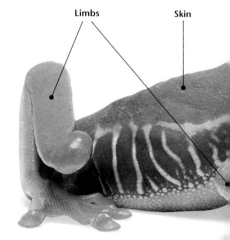

Limbs　　　　　　Skin

Eyes

Most species have good color vision. Movable eyelids protect the eyes of most frogs and salamanders. In land-living amphibians eyelids are necessary to stop the eye from drying out.

Tympanum

This is an eardrum visible in most frogs. Their hearing is well developed and they rely on calls when establishing territories and in attracting and finding a mate.

Tail

Only newts, salamanders, and larval amphibians have a tail, which is used for propulsion when swimming. The tails of terrestrial salamanders are often used in courtship and defense.

Skin

Skin is important in regulating water balance. Amphibians breathe through their skin and through their lungs. Their skin must be kept moist. Terrestrial species can easily become dehydrated. Most amphibians do not drink, but absorb moisture directly through their skin. Secretions in their skin help protect some species from drying out.

Skin colors can help the animal to blend in with its surroundings, warn predators that it is unpleasant or poisonous to eat, help it to establish a territory, or attract a mate. Skin also contains poison glands used for defense.

Sexual characteristics

- Cloaca. This is the opening for the amphibian's excretory and reproductive systems. In newts and salamanders, the male's cloaca becomes visibly more swollen than that of the female.
- Nuptial pads. When in breeding condition, male frogs and toads usually develop a dark patch of rough skin on their thumbs. These nuptial pads are used to help them grip onto the female's wet skin during mating.
- Vocal sac. Only male frogs and toads vocalize and produce calls by forcing air from their lungs into a vocal sac. The vocal sac, which expands during calling, is located in the throat.

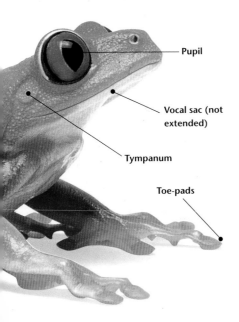

Pupil

Vocal sac (not extended)

Tympanum

Toe-pads

Caging

Housing amphibians correctly and creating the right environment can be time-consuming and expensive, but is the key to keeping them successfully. Your efforts will be well rewarded as you watch the inhabitants thrive in the habitat you have created.

Over the years, the equipment associated with the heating, lighting, and cleaning of aquaria has been very well developed. Also, as a result of the popularity of keeping reptiles, a large amount of suitable equipment for keeping terrestrial amphibians has become available.

Water

Amphibians absorb water directly through their skin. They sit in water and absorb it through their cloaca. For this reason, they must always have access to clean water, free from harmful additives. Many of the more terrestrial species require only a shallow container of clean water in which to hydrate. This must be replaced daily to avoid infections. If local water is not pure, use filtered or bottled water (but never distilled!).

For the more aquatic species, which spend most of their lives in water, the water used should not be too alkaline or acid, and should not contain excessive levels of chlorine or fluoride. There are additives available that remove chlorine. Various test kits are readily available for monitoring the pH (the alkalinity and acidity) and hardness of water. Most amphibians prefer a pH in the region of 6.5–7.5.

Maintaining water quality is most important and can be achieved in various ways. Normal aquarium filtration equipment will be adequate for most aquatic or semiaquatic setups, particularly if combined with regular water changes. A mechanical foam filter or undergravel filter should be installed, and, where not included, a small air pump should be used to oxygenate the water and help maintain water quality.

External Power Filter **Thermometer** **Thermostat** **Heat Pad** **Fluorescent Lighting**

Humidity

All amphibian environments need a certain level of humidity. One way of temporarily increasing the humidity in a vivarium is to spray it regularly with clean water from a plant mister. Better ways of permanently increasing the humidity are either to create constant running water with a circulating pump or by placing a small aquarium heater in the water section. You can also adjust the amount of ventilation. Try to avoid excessively high levels of humidity for long periods, as this seems to lead to health problems. Humidity can be measured using a hygrometer.

Heating

Many temperate and subtropical species can be kept at room temperature, which is normally around 15–20°C (60–68°F). Tropical species, which require a temperature between 20 and 27°C (68 and 82°F), will require additional heating. Thin heat pads linked to a thermostat can be positioned at the back or side of a terrestrial arrangement, and aquarium water heaters, which incorporate a thermostat, can be used in the aquatic

sections of most setups. Keep a thermometer inside the setup to accurately measure temperature. **Never use ceramic heaters or infrared bulbs with amphibians.**

Lighting

Most amphibians prefer subdued lighting. However, even nocturnal species need to have some "daylight" as this influences the animal's natural activities, including feeding routines. Plants will also need adequate light levels if they are to remain healthy. Lighting in the form of natural spectrum (high intensity) fluorescent tubes is best for amphibians. They provide ultraviolet light and little heat. Never use the "black-lights" recommended for keeping many reptiles, as these can seriously damage amphibian eyes and affect their general health. In aquaria, lighting can be mounted in hoods as long as they have been modified to allow for ventilation. With vivaria, fluorescent tubes can be mounted internally with waterproof fittings. Using a timer will assure consistent amounts of daylight.

Ventilation

Air circulation inside a vivarium is extremely important and is best accomplished and controlled by adjustable ventilation areas made of fine mesh or screen on the top and side or front. Heat from lights will cause the air inside to rise and this will in turn draw fresh air in from the lower vents. In aquaria, where no lower vent openings are available, an aerating pump or fan can be used to supply fresh air to the lower section.

Setups

Because the different types of amphibians have such a wide variety of requirements, matching them with the most suitable housing is very important. The following sections provide an overview of the different types of housings, their setup, and decoration. Throughout the book, dimensions of housing are given as length x height x width.

Most vivarium setups work best if they simulate the amphibians' natural habitat. With natural setups you can include a variety of living plants and natural floor coverings, or substrates, to make them visually interesting and attractive. The more elaborately furnished the setup, the more maintenance will be required. Whatever furnishings you use, the health

This inexpensive and hygienic type of accommodation is available in a range of sizes from most pet stores.

of your animal should be checked and its housing cleaned on a regular basis.

Plastic containers

The small plastic containers used for food storage, and clear plastic terraria types, make ideal homes for certain species. They are inexpensive, easily cleaned, and are particularly useful for rearing young and for the individual quarantining or treatment of a sick animal. Unfortunately, it is difficult to attach suitable heating and lighting to them.

Glass aquaria and vivaria

These are available in many different shapes and sizes. Traditional fish tanks are ideal for keeping fully aquatic species and can also be used successfully to house terrestrial or semiaquatic ones. Amphibians are great escape artists, so ensure that an escape-proof lid that incorporates an air vent is fitted. Custom vivaria that are designed with sliding glass access doors on the front and vents are the best housing for many amphibians. They work particularly well for semiaquatic, terrestrial, and also arboreal species that require tall vivaria with ventilation at the top and bottom.

Terrestrial

This setup is suitable for temperate or tropical ground-dwelling amphibians. Many of these can be quite secretive and should be provided with rocks or pieces of bark to hide under. Keep the substrate moist and maintain the humidity levels through regular mist spraying. Leaf-litter can be considered for using as a substrate, and a shallow water bowl should be placed in the vivarium.

Semiaquatic

This setup incorporates separate land and water sections. Where the species are fairly aquatic, and an aquarium is being used, a partition can be made of glass and the panels sealed into place using silicon sealer. An alternative is to create a shelf or platform over the water section. Other, more natural looking setups can be achieved by part filling the tank with substrate and simply allowing it to emerge from the water by various amounts. The size of the land area will depend on the species being kept and the amount of equipment necessary for filtering and aerating the water will depend on its volume. Semiaquatic setups can be used

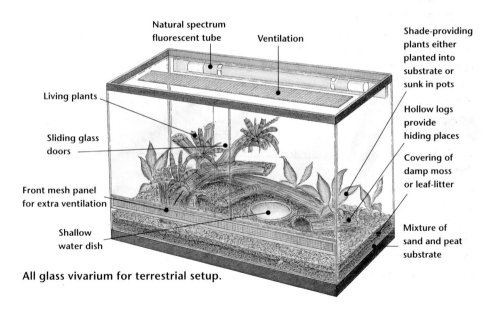

Natural spectrum fluorescent tube

Ventilation

Shade-providing plants either planted into substrate or sunk in pots

Living plants

Sliding glass doors

Front mesh panel for extra ventilation

Shallow water dish

Hollow logs provide hiding places

Covering of damp moss or leaf-litter

Mixture of sand and peat substrate

All glass vivarium for terrestrial setup.

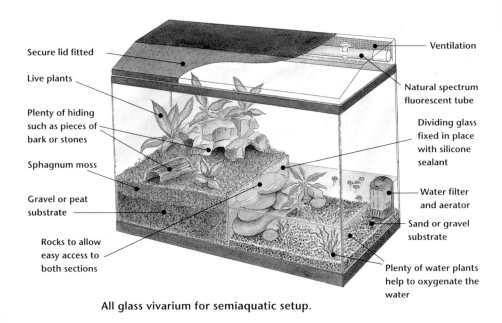

Secure lid fitted

Live plants

Plenty of hiding such as pieces of bark or stones

Sphagnum moss

Gravel or peat substrate

Rocks to allow easy access to both sections

Ventilation

Natural spectrum fluorescent tube

Dividing glass fixed in place with silicone sealant

Water filter and aerator

Sand or gravel substrate

Plenty of water plants help to oxygenate the water

All glass vivarium for semiaquatic setup.

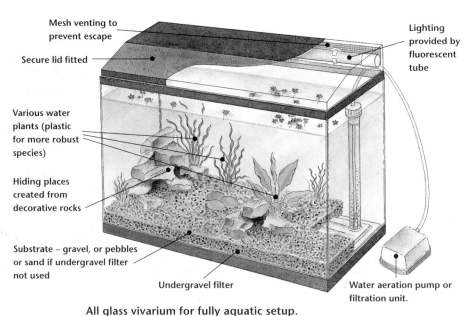

Mesh venting to prevent escape

Secure lid fitted

Various water plants (plastic for more robust species)

Hiding places created from decorative rocks

Substrate – gravel, or pebbles or sand if undergravel filter not used

Undergravel filter

Lighting provided by fluorescent tube

Water aeration pump or filtration unit.

All glass vivarium for fully aquatic setup.

Keeping Amphibians

for both temperate and tropical species, with higher temperature and humidity ranges being achieved by adding an aquarium heater to the water.

Fully aquatic

The equipment required for keeping aquatic amphibians differs little from that of fish-keeping. However, furnishings should be fairly sturdy. Gravel of various sizes can be mixed with pebbles to give a more natural looking substrate, and then stones can be strategically placed to create underground hiding places. Dead

leaves often look good as a substrate in aquatic frog tanks, especially if combined with waterlogged roots or dark bogwood. They will stain the water with tannic acid. Aquatic plants must be hardy; floating plants offer cover.

Semiarid

This setup will suit a number of toad species, which come from drier regions in both warm and temperate areas. Pebbles or rocks can be carefully arranged to give hiding places that still allow you to see the animal. The substrate should be allowed to

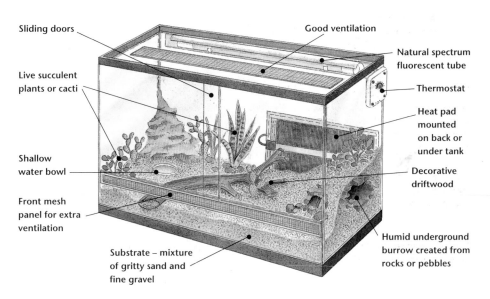

Sliding doors

Good ventilation

Natural spectrum fluorescent tube

Live succulent plants or cacti

Thermostat

Heat pad mounted on back or under tank

Shallow water bowl

Decorative driftwood

Front mesh panel for extra ventilation

Humid underground burrow created from rocks or pebbles

Substrate – mixture of gritty sand and fine gravel

All glass vivarium for semiarid setup.

retain a certain amount of moisture – the overall humidity is best maintained at about 50%. The surface can be made to look more appealing by decorating it with roots, driftwood branches, or imitation cacti. Live succulent plants can also be added. Provide a shallow bowl of clean water.

Most semiarid inhabitants prefer lower temperatures at nighttime than during the day, so you can use a rheostat or timer to decrease the lights and heating at night. Good ventilation is also very important; an extra vent in the lower part of the setup will increase the air-flow.

Arboreal

This setup is suitable for climbing amphibians, such as tree frogs, which benefit from living in a tall, planted vivarium. Many of these species need high humidity levels and this can be achieved by installing an aquarium circulating pump or by spraying. Running water will also increase the ventilation. Provide extra ventilation at the bottom, either by having a mesh vent strip in the side of the vivarium or by using an air pump. The interior back wall can be made from cork and covered with various live plants.

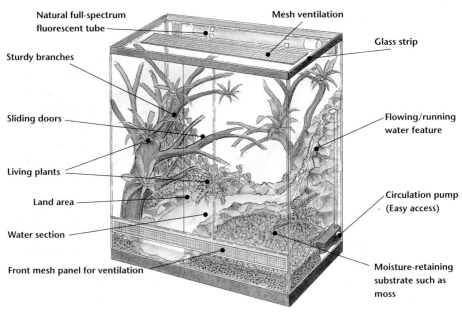

Natural full-spectrum fluorescent tube

Mesh ventilation

Glass strip

Sturdy branches

Sliding doors

Flowing/running water feature

Living plants

Land area

Circulation pump (Easy access)

Water section

Front mesh panel for ventilation

Moisture-retaining substrate such as moss

All glass vivarium for arboreal setup.

Other broad-leaved plants and sturdy climbing branches should be provided. It is advisable to have a glass lip around the edge of the top vent area to keep the animals from injuring their noses on the mesh when they climb the vertical surfaces. Natural spectrum fluorescent tubes will help maintain the condition of basking species and also promote plant growth. This setup works particularly well with subtropical and tropical species. The size and type of water container will depend on the species being kept. For some species, the base can be covered by water and aquatic plants encouraged to grow out of it. Others may have no need for a large water area, only requiring a shallow bowl that can be easily changed. For tropical species an aquarium heater and thermostat should be installed.

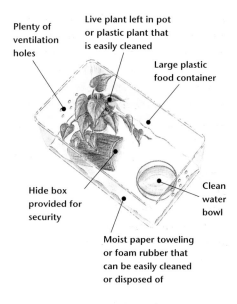

Plenty of ventilation holes

Live plant left in pot or plastic plant that is easily cleaned

Large plastic food container

Hide box provided for security

Clean water bowl

Moist paper toweling or foam rubber that can be easily cleaned or disposed of

Basic/simple setup.

Basic/Simple

This type of accommodation is ideal for amphibians that are in quarantine or for animals that need housing individually. It can also come in useful where space and maintenance time are limited or perhaps when temporary accommodation is required. Several types of containers including plastic shoe boxes, plastic food containers, and aquaria can all be used. Hygiene is a major consideration with this type of accommodation, so furnishings should be easily removed to allow efficient cleaning. The substrate should be able to retain moisture and be easily cleaned or replaced. This may consist of absorbent paper toweling, soft foam rubber, or sponge. Decorations should not be elaborate but should provide the amphibian with its basic requirements. Cork bark or a hide box will provide a hiding place for the animal to feel secure and an appropriately sized water container should also be added. The use of plastic plants can make simple terrestrial and aquatic setups look much more attractive. They can also be thoroughly cleaned (or sterilized) and re-used for quarantine purposes.

Feeding

To keep captive amphibians healthy, they should be provided with a varied diet that is nutritious and balanced. It is most important to ensure that the right size and amount of food is offered at the correct time.

Movement stimulates feeding for many amphibians, so in most cases the prey offered must be living. Aquatic species are highly sensitive to movement in the water or have a keen sense of smell. The sticky tongue of many terrestrial amphibians is attached at the front of the mouth, allowing it to extend out and catch prey with its sticky coating. Many amphibians, such as the tree frogs, actively seek out and stalk their prey. Others, like the Argentine Horned Frog, rely on camouflage to remain undetected and then grab anything the right size that goes past.

Availability

Local pet shops can often supply a wide range of live insects and prekilled food. There is also a growing number of mail-order companies that specialize in breeding insects for feeding amphibians. Other foods that are relished include spiders, beetles, and grasshoppers. These can be collected from outdoors, preferably in your garden, where you should be sure that they have not been sprayed with harmful insecticides.

Methods

Feeding times, and their frequency, will vary depending on the species concerned. Ideally, a nocturnal species should be offered food as soon as it becomes active. Feeding at this time will enable the animal to hunt down its food before it settles or hides. Most small species require feeding on a daily basis, while medium-sized species should be fed 3 or 4 times a week, and large species less frequently. The type and size of food also varies from species to species, and further information is given in the main text. As a general rule, the size of food offered should be no larger than the width of the amphibian's head. It is often difficult to judge how much to feed an amphibian and sometimes this can only be determined by trial and error. If the food offered is quickly devoured, then usually more can be added. If any uneaten food is left over, then the amount fed can be reduced accordingly. It is a good idea to place a stone or twig in the water area of your vivarium so that the insects do not drown. Remove any dead or uneaten food quickly, as this can soon foul the water and affect the health of your pet.

Greedy amphibians, like this young Horned Frog, grow very quickly if regularly offered nutritious food.

Live foods

Flies Flies are an excellent food for nearly all amphibians. They are cheap and easily obtained in their larval form, as maggots, from bait shops or through mail order. These normally pupate in a day or two and can then be separated into small batches. Raising the pupa at different temperatures will ensure a gradual supply of flies. The warmer the pupa are kept, the quicker they will develop. It is important that you remove any uneaten flies after feeding, as these may lay eggs under the amphibian's skin and harm it.

Crickets These are the most popular food offered to captive amphibians as they are very nutritious. Feeding crickets a specially formulated vitamin and mineral food supplement, and then dusting them with calcium powder prior to using them as food, will ensure that your amphibian gets a very healthy diet.

Care should be taken when feeding large adult or black field crickets to amphibians because these have strong biting mouthparts, which could cause harm. Female crickets may have a protruding spike at the rear, which is her ovipositor. It causes no harm.

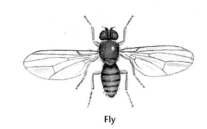

Fly

Mealworms and waxworms Mealworms are a favorite of many amphibians, including most salamanders and toads. However, they are difficult to digest and not very nutritious so should only be used sparingly to vary the captive diet. Waxworms are the larvae of the waxmoth. Although they are more nutritious and an excellent food for amphibians, they have only recently become available through specialist suppliers and can be expensive.

Black Field Cricket

Worms and slugs Most aquatic and semi-aquatic amphibians love to eat appropriate-sized earthworms. These can be dug from the garden, but be careful not to use the red manure worms, as these are distasteful and can even kill some amphibians. The small white or gray slugs that can also be collected from outdoors are a favorite food for many salamanders and newts. Avoid the larger species of slugs as they contain unpalatable secretions. Small bloodworms or tubifex are good food for many aquatic amphibians and are available from most pet shops.

Waxworm

Mealworm

(Illustrations not drawn to scale)

It is important to provide your amphibian with a varied diet.

Worms

Slugs

Mice

A number of large amphibians feed on prekilled mice. Your local pet shop may be able to offer you mice that have been humanely killed and frozen. Recently born mice are often called "pinkies."

Always defrost prekilled food thoroughly in warm water before offering it, and never refreeze any uneaten prekilled food.

Supplements

Several companies offer their own mixtures of essential vitamins and minerals for captive amphibians. Insects can be fed a highly nutritious food directly before they are fed to the amphibian, thus passing on the goodness, or the insects can simply be dusted with a vitamin and calcium powder prior to the feeding. The insect food products that contain pollen are highly recommended as these contain many of the trace elements normally found in the animals' natural diet. The regular dusting of insects with powders that have a high calcium content is also recommended, particularly for feeding to growing amphibians, which can soon develop deficiencies. Most aquatic amphibians are fed on naturally calcium-rich food and therefore require no supplement.

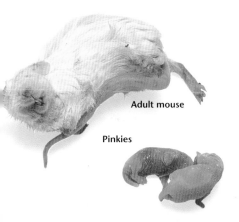

Adult mouse

Pinkies

Use a vitamin supplement to ensure you are giving a balanced diet.

Oriental Fire-bellied Toad

Bombina orientalis

Semiaquatic

Carnivorous

20 years

6 cm (2.5 in)

The Oriental Fire-bellied Toad comes from eastern Russia, Korea, and China. Here it lives around the edges of ponds and in ditches. In some areas it is also known to frequent paddy fields. It is incredibly colorful, having a bright grass-green upper surface, and a brilliant orange underside. It is also marked all over with black blotches and has bright orange finger and toe-tips matching the color of the belly. Males have slightly rougher skin than females, and their front legs are thicker. Females are more rounded than males.

This attractive and interesting toad makes a good choice of pet because it adapts very well to captivity and is active mainly during the day. It is one of the most commonly available amphibians and is easily kept under fairly simple conditions. "Fire-bellies" are usually bought as captive-bred toadlets (young

The colorful skin of a Fire-bellied Toad is covered with tiny glands containing toxic secretions.

The Fire-bellied Toad makes a good choice of pet because it adapts very well to captivity and is active mainly during the day.

Yellow-bellied Toad
Bombina variegata

Nostrils mounted high on the face allow the frog to breathe while it enjoys floating at the water's surface.

Male Fire-bellied Toads normally have shorter and thicker forearms than females.

From above, the orange toe-tips are the only sign that these toads have a toxic surprise in store.

toads) and, if cared for properly, will grow quickly and become fully grown at between 8 and 12 months old. Unfortunately, most of the toads that have been reared in captivity cannot produce the brilliant orange belly. This is due to the lack of color-producing compounds that occur naturally in their wild diet.

These active amphibians should be housed in a large aquarium or custom vivarium. Two or 3 pairs may be housed in a tank measuring 90 x 38 x 30 cm (36 x 15 x 12 in). A semiaquatic setup should be divided to incorporate a large shallow water section, filled to a depth of about 6 cm (2.5 in) with clean filtered water. Ideally, the water should be kept at a temperature of 20–24°C (68–75°F). Small-sized aquarium gravel makes a good substrate for both sections, but the land area should have a covering of damp moss to ensure that the toads do not eat the substrate by accident. Plenty of hiding places made from cork bark, rocks, or broken plant pots should also be provided. These toads enjoy sitting out under the lighting and should be given the opportunity to bask. Supplementary heating is not normally required, as the room temperature, together with the extra heat provided by the lighting during the day, should be sufficient. A drop in room temperature to 10–15°C (50–60°F) during the winter will be well tolerated, and may bring the toads into breeding condition.

The water section should contain a substrate of fine gravel and lots of water plants, such as *Elodea*. A land area can be arranged by positioning large stones or rocks so that the toads may climb easily in and out of the water. Substrate in the land section may include a covering of moss or may be planted with living plants. The attractive houseplant *Scindapsus* grows particularly well in wet situations, and needs little or no soil. Make sure that a well-ventilated and escape-proof lid is fitted to the tank, as these toads will escape if given the opportunity.

Being extremely aquatic, Fire-bellied Toads like nothing better than floating on the surface of the water with their legs outstretched. Apart from feeding on land,

they will readily take food from the water's surface, and may even dive below the surface in an effort to catch prey. Fire-bellies will feed on a variety of foods including crickets, waxworms, small earthworms, flies, and other small insects.

Regular handling of Fire-bellied Toads is not recommended. Although it is normally safe to do so, they do not enjoy it. Like other amphibians, their skin is delicate and also contains toxins. If it is necessary to handle your toads, hold them cupped between both hands or restrain them by grasping them around the upper part of the back legs while supporting their body. Do not handle them if you have cuts on your skin.

Fire-bellied Toads have strongly contrasting coloration, making them very attractive animals to keep.

Observation Point

Color

The most common method of defense for amphibians is camouflage. The color of its skin allows the amphibian to blend into the background (top right), whether that is green leaves high in the forest canopy or the brown leaf litter on the forest floor. However, colors can also serve another, quite different purpose. The amphibian may use color to advertise that it is distasteful or poisonous. Fire-bellied Toads use both these methods to increase their chances of survival. The colorful belly is used as a warning that they have harmful toxic secretions in their skin – when threatened, these toads arch their back downward, throw back their head, and raise the palms of their hands and feet to expose their bright color. This posture may be held for several minutes. If disturbed further, the toads may even flip over completely and freeze in a position which shows the whole of the brightly colored underside (bottom right). As a last resort they may secrete a milky fluid from glands in their skin, which is painful if it gets into your eyes.

Paddle-tailed Newt

Pachytriton labiatus

Aquatic

Carnivorous

20 years

18 cm (7 in)

The Paddle-tailed Newt is an interesting amphibian from southern China. It is a large, robust species, which is distinctly "chubby" in appearance. It has very smooth, slimy skin and, as its name suggests, has a broad tail, the sides of which are greatly flattened. Males may have a white blotch on their long tail, and use the tail to fan the female during courtship.

Extremely hardy and easy to maintain, this undemanding newt does very well in captivity. Apart from specialist suppliers, it may be available from many tropical fish shops. A large aquarium measuring about 90 x 38 x 30 cm (36 x 15 x 12 in) will provide ample space for a pair of newts. However, take special care not to put two males together as they are particularly aggressive creatures and highly territorial. Sometimes it can be difficult to determine the sex of an

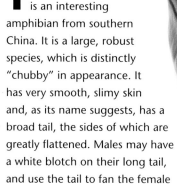

SIMILAR SPECIES
Spot-tailed Newt
Pachytriton brevipes

A wide, flattened tail helps the newt to swim against the current and is also used during courtship.

Female Paddle-tailed Newts are noticeably more rounded and stockier than the males.

The Paddle-tailed Newt is an aquatic, stream-dwelling amphibian, and makes a very unusual and interesting pet that is easy to keep.

amphibian, particularly if the animal is not fully mature. The sex of an adult newt can usually be determined from certain external characteristics. Female newts are noticeably more rounded and have a stockier build than the males, which can usually be identified by their more swollen cloacal region. Paddle-tailed Newts generally move more slowly than most other newts and tend to plod around on the substrate rather than swim. They are quite primitive-looking newts that seem almost prehistoric.

The newt's smooth, slimy skin is very delicate, so handling it is not recommended.

The eyes, set forward on the large flattened head, give the newt's face a short, rounded appearance.

This species requires clean filtered water that is very well oxygenated and, ideally, flowing. This can normally be achieved by using a mechanical canister-type filter or powerhead, incorporating a sponge and adjustable water flow. If mounted near the surface, this will allow water to aerate and to circulate across the tank to create a stream. The water level in the tank should be to a depth of at least 30 cm (12 in). Paddle-tailed Newts can stay submerged for very long periods without coming up for air. Occasionally you may even witness them snap with their wide mouths at the air bubbles produced by the filter or aquarium aerator, rather than take air at the surface.

Supplementary heating is not required for these newts, as they prefer cooler temperatures. A temperature of 15°C (60°F) is ideal for them, and a maximum temperature of 22°C (72°F) should not be exceeded. A window space in a cool part of the house can quite easily site the aquarium. Natural daylight will provide sufficient light levels for the newts, but take care that the aquarium does not receive direct sunlight, as this can quickly overheat it and harm the newts. Although it is not vital for the health of the newts, fluorescent lighting will enable close observation and enhance the look of the setup without producing too much heat. If artificial lighting is to be used, it is particularly important that you ensure the newts have shaded areas in which to take refuge. The top of the tank should be fully covered but well ventilated.

In the wild, Paddle-tailed Newts live in mountain streams where they spend their entire life in running water. Here they may be found living under rocks or large boulders. When maintaining them in captivity, it is best to try and replicate their natural environment by providing plenty of cover in the form of rocky hiding places. Pieces of slate can be angled with the

These newts are almost entirely aquatic, and it is important to provide them with a continual flow of cool, clean, and well-oxygenated water.

Observation Point

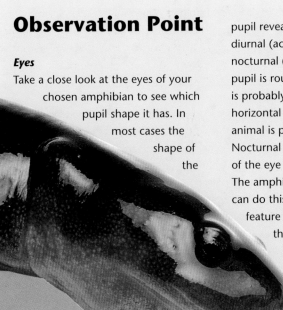

Eyes

Take a close look at the eyes of your chosen amphibian to see which pupil shape it has. In most cases the shape of the pupil reveals whether the animal is diurnal (active during the day) or nocturnal (active at night). If the pupil is round, the species in question is probably diurnal, and if it is horizontal or vertically elliptical, the animal is probably more nocturnal. Nocturnal species can close the pupil of the eye down when in bright light. The amphibians with vertical pupils can do this most effectively and this feature helps protect the retina in the eye from harmful ultraviolet rays during the day.

Recently it was discovered that the eyes of aquatic amphibians are able to rotate. As they angle their bodies upwards or downwards their eyes rotate so that they stay looking in the same direction.

water flow, and underwater "caves" can be created. Gravel, with a covering of small pebbles, works well as a substrate.

Paddle-tailed Newts are quite secretive animals, but at feeding time they will always come out and explore. They can sometimes become aggressive toward each other at this time, so if you have 2 newts housed together it may be better to feed them individually, one at each end of the aquarium. They eat a variety of small aquatic insects, bloodworms, and earthworms. It is best not to handle your newts, but if you need to transfer them from one container to another, use a net and great care to avoid injuring them.

Green Tree Frog

Hyla cinerea

Arboreal

Carnivorous

14 years

6.5 cm (2.5 in)

The Green Tree Frog comes from southeastern North America. Here it inhabits meadows and grasslands, particularly around still water such as ponds or lakes. As its name suggests, this frog is usually bright grass-green, but like many tree frogs it can change depending on its surroundings to yellow, brown, or a greenish-gray. It also has a clear light stripe running from its upper jaw along the side of its slender body. Males have a slightly darker and more wrinkled throat than females.

Most tree frogs including this species have expanded toe-pads, which enable them to climb more efficiently.

These beautiful little frogs are easily obtained and settle well into captivity. They require a tall arboreal setup, which should be

This popular and easily kept amphibian is one of the most frequently available of all the tree frog species.

Female Green Tree Frogs have paler and smoother throats than males.

Toe-pads on the hands and feet allow the tree frog to climb vertical glass surfaces of a vivarium with ease.

kept moist. A vivarium measuring 60 x 46 x 30 cm (24 x 18 x 12 in) will be plenty of space for at least 3 or 4 specimens. During the summer months the vivarium should be kept at a daytime temperature of 20–25°C (68–77°F), and this can drop at night down to about 18°C (65°F). Normal room temperatures should be suitable, even during the winter months when temperatures may be slightly cooler.

Lighting by natural spectrum fluorescent tubes will benefit the frogs and they may well bask under them during the day. Avoid using any type of incandescent bulb or spotlight inside the vivarium. If a frog jumps and lands on a hot light bulb it may fatally injure itself. Although a high level of humidity is required, good ventilation must also be provided. Mist spraying the

SIMILAR SPECIES

Squirrel Tree Frog
Hyla squirella

vivarium regularly will increase the humidity. A water bowl must be provided or, ideally, the bottom of the vivarium should be divided so that at least one quarter of it is water.

Decorations in the vivarium should include tree branches and, if possible, lots of live plants. Peat, covered by a fine layer of dead leaves or moss, can be used as a substrate for the land area. Cork bark often looks very effective at the back of an arboreal setup. It can provide places for the frogs to hide during the day and live plants can grow up it.

These frogs are primarily nocturnal and, when active, prefer to use their large toe-pads to climb around rather than jump. They do, however, relish the opportunity to stalk and jump after live flying food such as small flies and crickets. Feed your frogs every other night and use a powdered vitamin and calcium supplement on the insects.

Because these small delicate frogs are very fast and good jumpers, they are best left in their vivarium and handled only when necessary. If you wish to move them, it is best to do this quickly and to keep them contained within cupped wet hands.

The creamy-white stripe running along the flanks is probably this frog's most prominent characteristic.

Long legs help this agile frog to jump accurately when catching small flies and crickets.

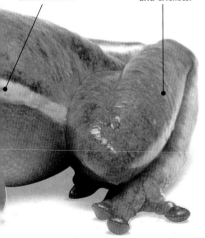

White's Tree Frog

Litoria caerulea

Arboreal/Simple

Carnivorous

15 years

11.5 cm
(4.5 in)

White's Tree Frog is a very large and rounded arboreal species that originated from rain forests in northeastern Australia and Indonesia. The frog's coloration can vary greatly depending on its surroundings. Its rubbery skin, waxy in appearance, may range from a pale or bright grass-green to blue or even chocolate-brown. White's Tree Frog has large feet and huge toe-pads, which support the frog's weight during climbing. The large Australian specimens tend to look particularly overweight and develop a thick fold of skin over their eardrum. The more slender Indonesian specimens, which are most commonly imported, are smaller and more agile than the Australian form. Adult males of both forms are generally much smaller than females and have gray, wrinkled throats and black nuptial pads during the breeding season.

This appealing frog makes an excellent pet. Its trusting and calm nature seems to make it naturally tame and it is easy to look after. It is one of the few amphibians that appears positively to enjoy being handled.

Most specimens are available as captive-bred froglets, usually about 2.5 cm (1 in) in size. These juveniles are easily raised in a simple setup. They should have a substrate of damp paper toweling, climbing branches, and a shallow water bowl. It is important that the housing is very well ventilated with vents or a small fan. A diet of crickets and flies should be offered almost daily and dusted with a vitamin/calcium supplement at every feeding. If fed well, the frogs will grow incredibly rapidly and may even be fully grown after 3 months.

White's Tree Frogs are best kept in groups and a tall arboreal vivarium measuring 100 x 50 x 50 cm (40 x 20 x 20 in) would be suitable for 4 or 5 adults. They prefer warm temperatures and should be maintained at 24–26°C (75–79°F) during the day with a drop to 20°C (68°F) at night. Supplemental heat can come from a heat pad mounted on the back of the vivarium. The vivarium must be well ventilated. Although these tree frogs are mainly nocturnal, they do enjoy basking under natural spectrum lighting during the day. They would benefit greatly from having two high intensity, natural spectrum

The "dumpy" look of these tree frogs adds to their appeal and gives the frogs "personality."

The skin, which is very smooth and waxy in appearance, helps the frog to retain moisture.

The high popularity of these large frogs is due to their calm and trusting nature and the fact that they are easy to look after.

Strong, muscular limbs enable these frogs to climb well and lead an arboreal life.

White's Tree Frogs often use their hands to help put food into their large mouths.

fluorescent tubes (such as Life-glo or Repti-sun), mounted inside the vivarium. The extra heat gained from basking seems to aid food digestion and help their growth.

Furnishings inside the setup should be kept sparse, as these frogs are quite messy. If a simple setup is used it is a good idea to have a substrate that can easily be removed and cleaned or replaced. A sheet of absorbent foam or sponge works well and can easily be dampened by mist spraying. Alternatively, artificial grass matting, available from most pet stores, can be cut to size and easily washed when necessary. For a more natural setup, a substrate consisting of a sheet of moss and a few large stones can be used. Never use gravel, bark chips, or small pebbles as they are likely to be swallowed by accident. Tree frogs like to be off the floor of the vivarium so plenty of thick

Like most tree frogs, the color of the skin may change from light green to chocolate brown, depending on the frog's mood and temperature.

White's Tree Frog uses its greatly enlarged toe-pads to adhere to surfaces and support its own body weight.

Observation Point

Sloughing

Frogs shed the dead outer layer of their skin every few days or so. This is called sloughing. It is very interesting to watch how they do this. First they open their mouth very wide, then arch their body to loosen the skin. They then eat their shed skin as it loosens from the body. If you are lucky, and watch closely, you should be able to observe your frog sloughing its skin and eating it. Frogs usually use their eyes when eating, tightly shutting

them when swallowing so that the eyeballs push down into the mouth to help force food down the throat.

sturdy branches should be carefully placed to enable them to bask under the lights. The use of a few easily washed plastic plants may enhance the overall appearance of the setup. A wide but shallow water bowl, just deep enough for the frogs to submerge themselves completely, must be provided and the water must be replaced daily.

White's Tree Frogs are very good feeders and unlike most nocturnal frogs they will wake up to take food during the day. They can be fed on large insects such as adult crickets and grasshoppers, which should be dusted with a vitamin and calcium supplement. Larger specimens will take small mice, but these should be offered only occasionally. Smaller frogs will also be eaten, so make sure that all specimens housed together are of similar sizes. It is best to feed White's Tree Frogs only 2 or 3 times a week. They are intelligent frogs and soon learn to take food directly from your fingers or forceps.

Tiger Salamander

Ambystoma tigrinum

Semiaquatic

Carnivorous

16 years

33 cm (13 in)

The Tiger Salamander is a North American species that lives in damp, humid habitats throughout most of the U.S.A., and as far south as Mexico.

This is the largest terrestrial salamander and one of the most variable. Some specimens are olive-green with lighter patches, spots, or stripes, while others are boldly marked with black and yellow bars. All have a broad head, small but prominent eyes with round pupils, and a tail that is long and flattened. Their wide mouth seems to be fixed in a permanent grin. Males can be distinguished by their swollen cloacal region, which is often surrounded by slightly frilly edging. Females are normally more rounded than males. Tiger Salamanders are only aquatic during the breeding season.

Tiger Salamanders are very easy to accommodate. They are best kept singly and require a medium to large semiaquatic setup.

A large mouth, equipped with teeth and a grooved tongue, helps this voracious feeder to overpower and devour its prey.

A vivarium measuring 90 x 38 x 30 cm (36 x 15 x 12 in) will be ideal for one individual. Section the tank to create half water and half land. The water level should be about 10 cm (4 in), or at least deep enough to let the salamander completely submerge itself. A substrate of sand can be used in the water section with pebbles leading to the land section.

The terrestrial section should have a damp substrate of potting

This attractive specimen shows typical markings of the eastern form of this salamander.

Many terrestrial salamanders use their tail in courtship, locomotion, or defense.

Small but prominent eyes have a round pupil characteristic of most salamanders.

provide hiding places for the salamander.

Normal room temperatures up to 23°C (74°F) during the day will suit these salamanders. Cooler nights and winter months will be naturally tolerated. A relatively high humidity of between 50 and 70% is best achieved through mist spraying, but the ventilation must also be good. As most salamanders prefer a darkened environment, special lighting is not required. Dim to moderate light levels provided by the lighting from the room will be sufficient.

Tiger Salamanders seem to positively enjoy being hand-fed. They are voracious eaters and should normally be fed at least twice a week or less if they are kept cool. They enjoy eating a wide variety of foods including earthworms, mealworms, waxworms, crickets, small slugs, and snails. Many will take the occasional prekilled small mouse if it is dangled in front of them with forceps. It is best to handle your salamander infrequently.

One of the better-known and more popular amphibians, Tiger Salamanders make interesting yet undemanding pets that thrive in captivity.

compost or peat substitute, suitable for the Tiger Salamander to burrow into, and be covered with spagnum moss or a deep layer of leaf litter. This substrate should always be kept moist. Wash or change biweekly. Placing tree bark on top of the moss or leaves will

SIMILAR SPECIES

Fire Salamander
Salamandra salamandra

Argentine Horned Frog

Ceratophrys ornata

Terrestrial/Simple

Carnivorous

15 years

18 cm (7 in)

Horned Frogs are weird-looking creatures, spectacularly colored, and easy to keep. For these reasons they are very popular and probably the most commonly kept of all amphibians. They get their common name from the short fleshy "horn" they have above each eye. There are 6 species of Horned Frog, all native to South America, but only a few of these are readily available and suitable for captivity. The Argentine Horned Frog, also known as Bell's or the Ornate Horned, is found in the pampas regions of Argentina, Uruguay, and Brazil. Commercial breeders have produced a variety of different color morphs, which are often referred to as "Pac-Man" Frogs or "Fantasy" Frogs. Albino forms are also commonly seen in the pet trade.

Horned Frogs are unmistakable in appearance. They have very wide bodies, and powerful but

The frog's short, stubby legs, which are useless for swimming, allow it to shuffle around.

The Horned Frog is a large and voracious amphibian that is hardy and very easily accommodated.

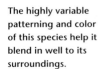

The highly variable patterning and color of this species help it blend in well to its surroundings.

For their relatively small size, the eyes of a Horned Frog give it exceptionally good vision.

short stubby legs, so they do not hop or swim well. The mouth of a Horned Frog is huge and almost as wide as its body. Being remarkably powerful and aggressive, the frog will attempt to overpower and eat prey almost as large as itself. In the wild it will eat small mammals, birds, and even other frogs. Should the frog be disturbed by a predator it will usually inflate its body to appear much larger. If threatened further, the fearless frog will lunge forward in attack with its mouth gaping.

Female Horned Frogs grow considerably larger than males. It is not possible to determine the sex of a juvenile Horned Frog and maturity is not reached until they are about 2 to 3 years old. Apart from their size, adult males can then be distinguished by their darker throat and the nuptial pads on the front feet, especially during the breeding season.

This frog's large mouth contains sharp, peg-like teeth, mounted on jaws that grip like a vise.

SIMILAR SPECIES

Cranwell's Horned Frog
Ceratophrys cranwelli

Care of this impressive amphibian is very simple. It requires subdued lighting and a constant temperature of 25–28°C (77–82°F). This temperature range should not be exceeded, but a slight drop in temperature at night should not be harmful. Heating is best achieved by background room temperatures, but if these are not high enough a heating pad can be mounted on the side of the tank.

This species is best kept singly and it will live quite happily in a small area. A single adult specimen can easily be housed in a tank measuring 46 x 30 x 30 cm (18 x 12 x 12 in). The setup must be easy

Close-up, the small, fleshy "horns" above the eyes are clearly visible, as well as the wide, gaping mouth that enables this frog to tackle large prey.

to clean on a regular basis, and it is best to limit the amount of furnishings. In a very simple setup, a plastic box or aquarium should contain a shallow water section and a land area made of rocks or foam for the frog to climb out on. The water depth should cover about half the frog, but must not cover its nostrils. In a natural vivarium setup, a deep substrate of gravel and leaf litter can be used and a log would make the frog feel secure. A shallow bathing dish should be provided and average humidity maintained by mist spraying every couple of days.

Cleanliness and proper feeding are very important when keeping Horned Frogs. With a good diet, conditions can quickly become dirty, so you should clean up after your frog every day or so following feeding. The water must be changed daily. When cleaning out your tank, care should be taken to lift the frog into another container. Although these frogs settle quickly and can be handled with ease, it should always be remembered that they are capable of giving a painful bite.

Horned Frogs are voracious feeders and have enormous appetites, but you must be careful not to overfeed your frog. Small frogs will normally take crickets, earthworms, and pinkie mice and should be fed 2 or 3 times a week. Growing froglets must be given regular vitamin and calcium supplements. Adults should be offered prekilled mice every 3 weeks. It is recommended that you use long forceps when offering food to any frog that bites.

Observation Point

Hide and seek!

Horned Frogs are masters of camouflage that have perfected a "sit and wait" strategy to help them feed, and also to avoid being eaten themselves. Their stocky, bright grass-green bodies are covered with a highly variable network of reddish-brown and yellow lines or blotches, which blend well with their surroundings. The eyes are set high on the frog's head, enabling it to completely burrow into the substrate with just its eyes and "horns" exposed. They lie in ambush, waiting for unsuspecting prey to pass.

You will know what your frog looks like, and where it is sitting, but it can be fun challenging your friends to spot your pet, and to see the look of amazement on their faces when they do!

Axolotl

Ambystoma mexicanum

Aquatic

Carnivorous

12 years

30 cm (12 in)

In the wild, Axolotls are found only in a few lakes in central Mexico. Here they have formed part of the diet of the people since the time of the Aztecs. Today, pollution and drainage threaten wild Axolotls. They are rare or absent from where they were once common, and wild Axolotls are now a protected species. In captivity, however, many are bred and raised successfully each year. They are a very interesting and popular animal.

Axolotls are normally dark grayish-brown or black in color, but pure white albino forms are not uncommon. They have large heads, wide mouths, and small eyes, which have no eyelids. A low crest along their back and tail helps them steer when swimming, but most of the time they prefer to walk about on the substrate.

The Axolotl is particularly unusual in that it is one of the few amphibian species that can live out its entire life cycle, while remaining

SIMILAR SPECIES

The larvae of the Tiger Salamander
Ambystoma tigrinum

in water, in a larval stage. The term for becoming an adult while still looking like a larva and being able to reproduce is "neoteny." Axolotls also have the amazing ability, shared with many other salamanders, to regenerate parts of their body that have been lost. They can grow back fully formed fingers, toes, and even whole limbs within a few weeks.

All the Axolotls that are available are captive-bred. Apart from reptile and amphibian dealers, they are also commonly available through tropical fish shops. Males can be recognized by their more slender body and swollen cloacal region. Females usually have shorter and slightly broader heads than males.

Axolotls are relatively easy to keep and are best accommodated in simple, large aquaria. In an enclosed area Axolotls will fight, but a pair can be housed quite happily in an aquarium measuring 76 x 46 x 38 cm (30 x 18 x 15 in). Most tap water is suitable for Axolotls and should be treated with an additive to remove the chlorine.

The water should be at least 30–46 cm (12–18 in) deep. The setup should be equipped with a basic aerator, and, most importantly, a good foam filter. Maintaining the water quality is very important and filtration should be supplemented by regular water changes.

Native only to a few lakes in Mexico, this popular salamander is a protected species, but is available entirely from captive-bred stocks.

Their small eyes are very sensitive, and they have no protective eyelids, so Axolotls prefer to live in low light.

These salamanders can be obtained in several different colors, including this white albino form.

Axolotls are able to grow back fingers, toes, and even whole limbs within a short periods of time.

By hand-feeding Axolotls, usually using forceps, you will be able to monitor accurately the appetite and individual food requirements of your pets.

Any large particles of solid waste or uneaten food need to be removed or the water will quickly foul.

Axolotls are very tolerant of wide temperature ranges and do well at room temperatures of 10–25°C (50–77°F). Normal room lighting will be sufficient. Axolotls are much more active in dim light. They have no eyelids to protect them from harsh lights, so if you use aquarium lighting be sure to provide areas where the animals can shelter themselves.

Use large aquarium gravel as a substrate and a few large pebbles or rocks for decoration and hiding places. The setup can be made more attractive by adding plants, but these must be very robust or they will easily be uprooted. Good quality plastic plants can be very

life-like and are probably the best choice.

Wild Axolotls usually feed at night and are aggressive feeders. When hungry, they will sometimes attack and bite off the limbs and gills of other Axolotls. Captive Axolotls do well if fed on earthworms, small fish, and thin strips of raw lean meat. Large adults will sometimes take pinkie mice. They can be fed as often as 3 times a week, depending on the water temperature, but do not overfeed or allow any uneaten food to remain in the tank. Use forceps to move the food in front of the Axolotl until it snaps at it with its large gaping mouth.

Axolotls should only be handled when they need to be transferred to another container. A large net should be used to trap them, and then they should be grasped firmly but gently with two hands. One should be placed around the neck and shoulders, the other around the legs and tail. Axolotls have soft bones and can be damaged easily, so handle them gently, do not squeeze them too tightly, and be careful of their gills.

When releasing an Axolotl into new surroundings, ensure that the water is at a similar temperature to the water from which it is being transferred.

Observation Point

Gills

Axolotls obtain oxygen through their skin and also through well-developed external gills. Young Axolotls are more active than adults and obtain the high levels of oxygen they need by having large gills. As they grow, and become less active, their oxygen requirement reduces. Look carefully at your Axolotl and note the size of the feathery gills it has on either side of its head. The size of the gills also varies according to the temperature of the water in which the Axolotl is kept. The gills are largest in adults that are kept in warm water, since this contains less oxygen than water at lower temperatures. Adults may increase their oxygen intake by rising to the surface to gulp air.

African Clawed Frog

Xenopus laevis

Aquatic

Carnivorous

15 years

14 cm (5.5 in)

In the wild, African Clawed Frogs live in slow-moving streams and ponds. Their small eyes are set high on top of the head so that they can watch for predators at the water's surface. They have flattened bodies, strong, muscular legs, and large feet that are fully webbed and well adapted for swimming. Their toes have sharp claws, from which they get their common name. Usually, clawed frogs are mottled grayish-brown with white undersides. Albino forms are also commonly seen in captivity, and these are often called "Golden Clawed Frogs." Females are larger than males and have three small folds of skin around the cloaca.

African Clawed Frogs are totally aquatic pets that do extremely well in captivity and are readily available from tropical fish shops. A pair can be comfortably accommodated in a standard glass aquarium measuring 60 x 30 x 40 cm (24 x 12 x 16 in). The top

of the aquarium should be completely covered with a well-ventilated and escape-proof lid. A good level of light should be provided, and sometimes the frogs will bask motionless on the surface, directly under the fluorescent lights.

African Clawed Frogs are very tolerant of a wide range of temperatures. The water should be at least 20 cm (8 in) deep, and an aquarium heater and thermostat should be used to maintain it at a temperature of 22–27°C (72–81°F). A good quality filter will be essential to keep the water as clean as possible. An undergravel or foam filter will prevent the buildup of some toxins, but regular partial water changes will also be necessary. Complete water changes should also be done every couple of months.

Furnishings in the aquarium can be as elaborate as you wish to make them. A layer of fine sand or gravel can be used as a substrate, with rocks and artificial plants enhancing a basic setup. An alternative may be to use dead leaves on the bottom of the tank. Use pieces of bogwood to enhance the natural appearance, and a foam cannister filter.

African Clawed Frogs are greedy and very easy to feed. They will tackle nearly anything moving on or below the water's surface that will fit into their wide mouths. Earthworms and a variety of insects will be readily accepted. Feeding them 2 or 3 times a week should be sufficient. Any uneaten food must be removed to keep the water clean. Never handle clawed frogs, and use a net when transferring them to other containers.

Large webs on the back feet can propel the frog forward or backward very quickly.

A row of highly sensitive receptors along the frog's body help it to detect changes in its environment.

Small, protruding eyes, widely set at the top of the head, help the frog to peer above the water's surface.

Sensitive fingers detect the movement of prey in the water, and help to cram food into the mouth.

This interesting and totally aquatic amphibian is easy to care for and does extremely well in captivity. It can escape readily if the cage top is not secure.

Red-spotted Newt

Notophthalmus viridescens

Semiaquatic/
aquatic

Carnivorous

10 years

12 cm (5 in)

Red-spotted Newts are quite common throughout eastern North America. They are very unusual in that the juveniles, which are known as red efts, are remarkably different than the adults. Efts have a rough skin texture and are bright orange or red all over, and are usually very terrestrial. They reach maturity at 2 to 4 years and then, as adults, spend most of their time in the water. The adults are smooth-skinned and olive-green above. They have dark-bordered red spots along each side of the body, and a pale yellow underside. Adult males develop a beautiful crest above and below their tail in the breeding season.

Red-spotted Newts are often available in pet shops and from specialist reptile and amphibian suppliers. They are hardy and adapt well to captivity. Several newts can be housed together in an aquarium measuring 60 x 38 x 30 cm (25 x 15 x 12 in). The top of the aquarium should be fitted with a well-ventilated and escape-proof lid. These newts seem content to live at room temperatures between 18 and 22°C (65 and 72°F). The tank should be sited in natural light, but not in direct sunlight. Alternatively, use natural spectrum fluorescent tubes to improve the look of the tank, and to promote good plant growth within it.

Habitat preferences change as the newts develop from red efts to mature adults. Efts require a

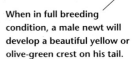

When in full breeding condition, a male newt will develop a beautiful yellow or olive-green crest on his tail.

An interesting and attractive species, this newt is easy to acquire and will live for a long time if cared for properly.

Black-spotted Newt
Notophthalmus meridionalis

medium-sized semiaquatic setup with plenty of damp places to hide. Peat can be used as a substrate and covered with a fine pillow of green moss or damp leaf litter. Pieces of bark, broken plant pots, or a hollow log may all serve as hiding places. A water section should still be provided, but this need not be as deep as for the adults.

A mainly aquatic setup is required for adult Red-spotted Newts. Occasionally they like to come out of the water and should be given something to climb out onto, such as a floating moss-covered

platform made of polystyrene or cork bark. The water, which should always be very clean and well oxygenated, should reach a depth of at least 15–23 cm (6–9 in). It is recommended that an undergravel filtration system be installed, and that plenty of oxygenating plants, such as *Elodea*, be used to maintain water quality.

These newts are excellent hunters and will continually be on the lookout for food above or below the water surface. Offer a variety of foods, including small worms, small waxworms, bloodworms, crickets, and other small insects.

If handled roughly, these newts can secrete a toxin that can cause skin irritation. Do not handle newts and then rub your eyes, nose, or mouth. Rather than handling them, use a net when transferring them from one container to another. If you have to handle these newts, do so gently and wash your hands immediately afterwards.

These newts have small, elongated lungs, and their wet skin acts as an additional area for respiration.

This adult, unlike a juvenile, should be housed in an almost completely aquatic setup.

When disturbed or threatened, these newts secrete toxins, so wash your hands immediately after handling them.

Western Green Toad

Bufo debilis

Semiarid

Carnivorous

3 years

5.4 cm (2 in)

The Western Green Toad lives in the drier regions of North America. Here it spends most of the day sheltering under rocks as well as in burrows. It prefers habitats with loose soil in which it can dig. It emerges mainly at night to feed and look for breeding sites.

This small, secretive amphibian is one of the most attractive of all the toads. Its bright yellowish-green skin is covered with an irregular network of fine black spots that fuse in places to form intricate patterns. The legs are marked with black bars. It has a short broad head and a flatter body than many other toads. The sexes can be easily told apart; males have a dark gray throat while the female's throat is cream to light yellow.

Western Green Toads are readily available and fairly undemanding in captivity. Sometimes they can take a while to settle into their new surroundings, but once accustomed, they do very well.

They require a semiarid vivarium with daytime temperatures of 20–25°C (68–77°F). Ventilation

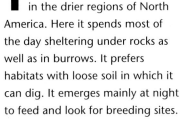

The skin is covered with an intricate pattern, making the toad particularly well camouflaged.

Although this attractive small toad can be quite secretive at times, it makes a very interesting pet once it has overcome its nervousness.

must be good. A pair of Western Green Toads can be housed in a vivarium or aquarium measuring 46 x 30 x 30 cm (18 x 12 x 12 in). At first, cover the vivarium so that the toads cannot see out, or they may jump at the glass in attempts to escape. They will soon calm down and the covering can be removed.

When threatened, the toad flattens itself to the ground in an effort to remain undetected.

The Western Green Toad has short, sturdy limbs that help it to burrow into the soil.

The parotoid glands, located behind the head, contain secretions used in defense.

Sandy soil should be used as a substrate, with part of it kept moist. Provide lots of places for the toads to burrow and hide. These could include cork bark, half flowerpots filled with loose soil, or rocks bridged by slate or a large flat stone. Also provide a flat dish of clean water. Place a small stone or piece of wood in the dish so the toad will be able to enter and leave the water more easily. Fluorescent tubes can be used as lighting over the setup and although the toads are mainly nocturnal, once they have become bold, they may come out into the open to bask or feed during the day.

These toads will take crickets of approximately 3–4 mm (0.15 in) in size. If crickets are to form the main part of the diet, they must be regularly dusted with a vitamin and calcium supplement. Western Green Toads also love waxworms, mealworms, and small beetles.

These toads are easily stressed. The less they are handled, the more secure they feel. An undisturbed toad that has settled into its surroundings is also more likely to behave naturally.

Couch's Spadefoot Toad

Scaphiopus couchii

Semiarid

Carnivorous

12 years

9 cm (3.5 in)

There are 6 species of Spadefoot Toad, but Couch's is the most attractive. The males are fairly plainly marked but the females are yellow and have chocolate-brown mottled markings. Their undersides are creamy-white. These toads have large golden eyes, which have a vertical pupil, and a sharp bony "spade" on their foot, which helps them to dig, and from which they get their common name. They can easily create a burrow with it by shuffling backwards into loose soil.

Spadefoot Toads can survive very dry conditions for long periods. Couch's Spadefoot Toad is a western North American species, which comes from quite a dry environment. It burrows deep down into the sand and soil for many months to avoid drying out and then protects itself from drying out completely by making a cocoon around it out of dead skin.

Spadefoot Toads breed after coming to the surface when the heavy rainstorms come. The males have a very loud call, sounding similar to the bleat of a lamb, which is used to attract females. They deposit their eggs on plant stems over only 2 or 3 nights and the tadpoles hatch within 20 hours. These develop very rapidly before the pools dry out. Taking only about 15 days to change into tiny froglets, they are among the most rapidly developing of all tadpoles.

This species requires a medium-sized semiarid vivarium, about 46 x 30 x 30 cm (18 x 12 x 12 in), which should be kept at a daytime temperature of 25–30°C (77–86°F). Link the heat pad, mounted on the back of the vivarium, to a rheostat or timer to reduce the temperature at night to around 20°C (68°F).

SIMILAR SPECIES

Western American Spadefoot
Scaphiopus hammondi

Being highly secretive, Couch's Spadefoot Toad would benefit greatly from the specially constructed underground burrow highlighted in the caging section (p. 15). A deep layer of substrate consisting of sandy soil and fine grit should be used and this should incorporate both a dry and moist area. A shallow water container must also be provided.

In the wild, Couch's Spadefoot Toad also times its emergence with the swarming of termites on which it feeds. In captivity it is mainly nocturnal, and will spend most of the day tucked into its burrow. However, at night it quite often emerges from its hiding place to eat small insects such as crickets and waxworms.

These toads have a secretive nature and do not like to be disturbed. They should only be handled when it is really necessary to move them. Handle them quickly but securely with damp hands.

Reaching 9 cm (3.5 in), this female is considerably larger and more colorful than a male.

The vertical pupil becomes wide and rounded at night to enhance the toad's vision.

This species is the most readily available and one of the most attractive of all the Spadefoot Toads.

In order to keep these secretive toads successfully you need to provide a semiarid vivarium with plenty of soft material for the toad to burrow in.

The strong back legs are used to displace loose soil as the frog shuffles back into its burrow.

Marbled Reed Frog

Hyperolius marmorata

Arboreal/
semiaquatic

Carnivorous

5 years

3 cm (1.1 in)

The Marbled Reed Frog is an African species that occurs in a wide variety of colors and markings. Although many of these highly colorful frogs are marbled, some can be striped or spotted. Their underside is white to yellow in color and the thighs, as well as the palms and soles, are red. Males have a round disk-shaped bulge in the center of bright yellow throats.

As their common name implies, these small arboreal frogs normally live in the humid vegetation around ponds, lakes, and swamps. In captivity, a large group can quite easily be maintained in a small to medium arboreal vivarium measuring 60 x 46 x 30 cm (24 x 18 x 12 in). The bottom of the vivarium should have a large area of water, ideally with tall aquatic plants emerging from it. The land section can have peat covered with moss as a substrate. Live plants such as *Scindapsus* or *Spathiphylum* species should be added to this section. A network of small

Reed frogs vary in pattern and coloration, but the red hands and feet are typical of this particular species.

Native to Africa, these small, brightly colored frogs can be housed with ease, and will thrive in captivity if given the right environment.

branches should be supplied for the frogs to climb.

A moist environment in the vivarium should be maintained through regular mist spraying. The daytime temperature should be kept constant at between 22–28°C (72–82°F), but a slight drop in temperature at night, down to no less than 18°C (65°F), will be tolerated. Temperature levels can be achieved by a heat pad mounted on the back or side of the vivarium. Lighting is best supplied by fluorescent tubes.

These small and delicate amphibians are exceptionally sensitive to unclean surroundings.

Catch these agile frogs only when necessary and keep them securely enclosed in your hand.

Reed frogs should always be quarantined before introducing them to your collection.

During the day these frogs tend to sit on leaves or perch in the top corners of the vivarium with their legs and arms pulled tightly against their bodies. If you mist spray them early in the evening, they will soon become active and alert, moving around using their sticky finger and toe-pads to help them climb.

Reed Frogs will readily accept small crickets, and especially flies, which should be dusted with a vitamin and calcium supplement. Spiders and small insects that can be collected during the summer months will be relished and are particularly nutritious. Although the frogs are mainly nocturnal they will sometimes feed if presented with food during the day. Avoid handling your Reed Frogs unless it is really necessary to move them, as they escape very easily.

Great care should be taken when introducing new frogs to your group. These frogs easily catch bacterial infections, which can be fatal, so several weeks of strict quarantine should be given to any new animals you get, and the vivarium should be cleaned very regularly. It is also vital to keep the water in the vivarium very clean.

SIMILAR SPECIES

Clown Reed Frog
Afrixalus dorsalis

Red-eyed Leaf Frog

Agalychnis callidryas

Arboreal

Carnivorous

12 years

8 cm (3 in)

Red-eyed Leaf Frogs look spectacular, and are one of the most interesting amphibians you can keep. The frog has a bright green back and legs, and the sides range from vivid purple to sky-blue in color and are striped with creamy-white bars. They have orange hands and feet and bright red eyes. They are found in the humid tropical rain forests of Central America.

Keeping Red-eyed Leaf Frogs is not easy, and it is best to have had some experience caring for other tree frogs before keeping them. They require a medium to large, tall vivarium. A group of 3 or 4 adults is best housed in a vivarium at least 60 x 60 x 38 cm (24 x 24 x 15 in). Being a tropical species, they must always be kept warm. A temperature of 25–30°C (77–86°F) should be maintained during the day, with a drop to about 18°C (65°F) at night. A heat pad attached to the side of the vivarium may be necessary to achieve the required temperature.

SIMILAR SPECIES

Spurrell's Leaf Frog
Agalychnis spurrelli

The color and patterning along the flanks of Red-eyed Leaf Frogs vary depending on where they are from.

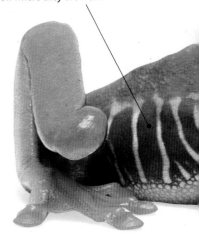

This is one of the most beautiful of all the amphibians, but should only be considered as a pet by the more experienced enthusiast.

Ventilation is very important. Humidity in the vivarium during the day can be as low as 50%, but you can increase this at night by lightly mist spraying. Try to keep the humidity between 50–80%, as levels above this for long periods may lead to health problems. Attaining the correct balance between the temperature, ventilation, and humidity is the key to keeping this species successfully.

A water section should always be available to the frogs. This may be as simple as a shallow water container, but it is vital that the water is kept clean. If possible, use bottled or filtered water and change it daily. Dirty water will soon spread fatal infections. An arboreal setup for these frogs should be furnished with branches to climb and preferably real plants such as *Scindapsus, Phyllodendron,* and *Monstera,* which are hardy, sturdy, and have wide leaves. The plants can either be left in their pots or directly planted into a natural substrate. Be careful not to use moss or a material that may stick to the frog's skin, or be accidentally swallowed. This can cause distress to the frogs and harm them. A more practical alternative, as long as the humidity levels can be maintained, is to leave the floor of the vivarium bare. This may not look very attractive, but it is much easier to clean and could therefore prevent the spread of infection.

In the wild, leaf frogs typically breed in bushes and trees, where they attach their eggs

Watching the activity of these nocturnal frogs provides valuable insight into their unusual lives.

A vertical pupil is a typical characteristic of all Leaf Frogs. This species has beautiful bright red eyes.

Opposable fingers and toes enable this species to grip branches and climb with ease.

to leaves overhanging water. Captive breeding requires a large vivarium with a pool section.

Red-eyed Leaf Frogs are strictly nocturnal and will spend the day tucked away on the underside of a leaf or resting in the corner of the vivarium; they should be disturbed as little as possible. Although these frogs are nocturnal, lighting the setup with a natural spectrum fluorescent tube during the day should be considered. This will benefit the frogs and will promote plant growth. At night the frogs become active, begin to move around, and start

Completely concealed at rest, the fantastic coloration of this species never fails to amaze when the frog is on the move.

feeding. In captivity, the frogs will feed on insects such as moths or crickets, dusted with a calcium and vitamin supplement. Each frog should be fed approximately 3 to 4 crickets, 2 or 3 times a week. Handle these frogs only when necessary: they have extremely delicate skin and they are very good at jumping.

Young Red-eyed Leaf Frogs are best purchased when they are at least 2 cm (1 in) long and look like perfect miniature versions of the adults. At this size they should be housed in small plastic terrariums, and maintained under similar conditions to the adults. The bottom of the container should be covered with a layer of paper toweling, which must be changed regularly. It should be kept damp to

Observation Point

Webbing

The amount of webbing between the toes of frogs varies between species. Most frogs have little or no webbing on the front feet. However, the other extreme is seen in several tree frog species from Central America to Southeast Asia. Their hands and feet have developed such heavy webbing that they are able to glide between trees. All leaf frogs have webbing between their toes, and this feature helps them to jump further or "parachute" down from the tree canopy.

maintain a certain amount of humidity. When raising small frogs it is usually best to encourage them to feed more frequently than adults. Appropriate-sized crickets should be offered, but care should be taken not to put too many insects in the container as this can stress the frogs. Providing twigs for the small insects to climb will increase feeding opportunities. The size of the container should be increased as the frogs grow. If kept under the correct conditions these frogs grow quickly, reaching maturity in 12 months.

When handling these frogs, it is best to let them perch on your fingers or sit on the back of the hand, rather than holding them.

Record Card

Recording information can give you a more complete picture of your pet. It can enable you to identify individuals, and even spot unusual behavior that may indicate ill health. Through record keeping, casual observations easily develop into interesting personal studies, adding real value to keeping your pet.

Start by monitoring the environment that your pet is going to live in. It is a good idea to keep a regular note of the temperature and humidity levels at different times of the day and night. When you obtain your animal, measure its size and note the date it was purchased. You may wish to photograph, sketch, or note any distinguishing markings that will help you to identify the individual. Also record how much and how frequently it is eating until you feel confident of its feeding requirements.

Recording the daily activities of your pet and noting any unusual observations on a record card can easily develop into an in-depth personal study. If you do observe something of particular interest, it is a good idea to write it down on the spot rather than leave it until later. Remember that nothing is too insignificant to be noted down and that collecting sufficient information to get a complete picture of your pet cannot be done all at once. There will be many new things to discover about your pet so you may take notes over several months or even years.

Record Card

Species _____   Temperature_____

Name _____   Humidity_____

Size _____   Preferred foods _____
_____
Date purchased _____   _____

Date	Event	Notes
e.g., for a tree frog		
April 14	feeding	Lights off at 8 P.M., lightly spray-misted vivarium, and she started moving around at 8:20, fed on 6 vitamin-dusted crickets between 8:30 and 9 P.M.
April 16	shedding skin	Observed her sitting in humid area at back right-hand corner of vivarium (same place as last time) – 10:30 P.M. Started to stretch and open mouth at 10:45. By 10:52 P.M. shed skin had been completely eaten and she moved directly into clean water bowl.
April 19	feeding	She sat on a favorite leaf all day. 9:30 P.M. – 8 crickets eaten, nuptial pads starting to become prominent; she must be a male!

Amphibians Quiz

How well do you know your amphibian?

Test your knowledge with the quiz below.

1. Can you give two good reasons why it is preferable to obtain captive-bred amphibians?

2. What term is used to describe the eardrum of a frog?

3. How can you ensure your pet is receiving essential vitamins and minerals?

4. What feature do tree frogs possess that enables them to climb with ease?

5. Which colorful amphibian has a vertical pupil in the eye?

6. Which amphibian has a grin like a Cheshire cat, but is named after a bigger cat, and why?

7. What do frogs do with the skin they shed?

8. Which species of frog has a mouth that is almost as wide as its body and can give a painful bite?

9. Which amphibian's natural habitat is restricted to only a few lakes in Mexico?

10. Which species of newt is bright red when young and as an adult spends most of its time in water?

11. Which primitive toad can survive very dry periods by digging underground?

12. Apart from swimming, how do some frogs use the webs between their toes?

Answers

1. (i) It helps reduce the number collected from the wild, and (ii) they are usually free from parasites and more healthy. 2. A tympanum. 3. Use a food supplement. 4. Large toe-pads. 5. Red-eyed Leaf Frog. 6. Tiger Salamander, because it is striped and has an appetite like a tiger. 7. They eat it. 8. Horned Frog. 9. Axolotl. 10. Red-spotted Newt. 11. Spadefoot Toad. 12. To glide between trees.

Useful Information

Societies

The Society for the Study of Reptiles and Amphibians
Dept. of Zoology
Miami University
Oxford, OH 45056
(Publishes *Herpetological Review* and *The Journal of Herpetology*)

The American Society of Ichthyologists and Herpetologists
Dept. of Zoology
Southern Illinois University
Carbondale, IL 62901-6501
(Publishes *Copeia*)

Herpetologists' League
Maureen A. Donnelly
College of Arts and Sciences
Florida International University
North Miami, FL 33181
(Publishes *Herpetologica*)

Magazines

Reptiles Magazine
Fancy Publications, Inc.
PO Box 58700
Boulder, CO 80322

Reptile and Amphibian Hobbyist
One TFH Plaza
Neptune City, NJ 07753

On-line Sources

Here are some good addresses:

One of the biggest and best-linked reptile/amphibian sites is at Kingsnake.com

Sites that deal with amphibian care include the following:

http://www.icomm.ca/dragon/careshts.html
http://www.sonic.net/melissk/mainamphibian.html
http://www.acmepet.com/reptile/library/he_educ.html
http://www-personal.umich.edu/~morbius/newt.html
http://www.newts.org/~nootnerd/index.html
http://www.syspac.com/~varney/NETSCAPE/caresheet/tigersal.html
http://www.total.net/~kaymur/salmr5.htm
http://www.ci.austin.txus/aquifer/amphib.htm
www.wcu.edu/hibio

Books

Frogs, Toads and Treefrogs by R.D. Bartlett and Patricia Bartlett (Barron's Educational Series, Inc., Hauppauge, NY, 1996).

Newts and Salamanders by Frank Indiviglio (Barron's Educational Series, Inc., Hauppauge, NY, 1997).

A Field Guide to Reptiles and Amphibians of the Eastern and Central North America by Roger Conant (Houghton Mifflin, Boston, MA, 1998).

A Field Guide to Western Reptiles and Amphibians by Robert C. Stebbins (Houghton Mifflin, Boston, MA, 1985).

Care and Breeding of Popular Tree Frogs by Phillippe de Vosjoli, Robert Mailloux, and Drew Ready (Advanced Vivarium Systems, Inc., Santee, CA, 1996).

Index